The Tech Diet:

Finding Balance in a Hyperconnected World

By

Leah Wong

TABLE OF CONTENTS

CHAPTER I
Introduction

A. The Technology Paradox: The blessings and curses of hyperconnectivity

In the digital age, the world has witnessed an unprecedented surge in hyperconnectivity. With the proliferation of smartphones, social media platforms, and smart devices, we are constantly bombarded with a plethora of information and interactions. While this interconnectedness has undoubtedly revolutionized the way we live, work, and communicate, it has also brought along a paradoxical reality – the blessings and curses of hyperconnectivity.

The blessings are evident and awe-inspiring. The ability to connect with people from every corner of the globe in an instant has transcended barriers of time and space. Long-lost friends are rediscovered, families separated by miles are brought together, and collaborative opportunities have expanded exponentially. Hyperconnectivity has democratized knowledge, allowing individuals to access information and education like never before. It has enabled breakthroughs in medicine, science, and technology, empowering humanity to confront global challenges and create innovative solutions.

Yet, amid these blessings lies a subtler narrative - the curses of hyperconnectivity. As we are constantly immersed in the digital world, our attention is fractured and divided. Distractions lurk around every corner, and the allure of instant gratification hinders our ability to concentrate deeply on meaningful tasks. The pervasive nature of technology has blurred the boundaries between work and leisure, leading to an "always-on" mentality that can drain our mental and emotional well-being.

Moreover, the rise of social media and the never-ending comparison game have given birth to a new form of anxiety - the fear of missing out (FOMO). We find ourselves tethered to virtual validation, seeking affirmation from others in the form of likes, comments, and shares. This constant pursuit of external validation can erode our self-esteem and breed a sense of inadequacy.

Furthermore, the incessant exposure to information, much of it polarizing and emotionally charged, can take a toll on our mental health. The overwhelming barrage of news, updates, and notifications can induce stress and contribute to the rising phenomenon of technostress. This can lead to burnout, anxiety, and a diminished ability to cope with life's challenges.

The need to find balance in this hyperconnected world is becoming increasingly urgent. We must acknowledge both the tremendous potential and the unintended consequences of our technology-infused lives. As we delve into "The Tech Diet," we embark on a journey to explore ways to embrace the blessings of hyperconnectivity while mitigating its curses. It is not a call to abandon technology altogether but rather to develop a mindful and purposeful relationship with it.

By understanding the Technology Paradox, we can begin to unravel the complexities of our digital existence and uncover practical strategies to restore equilibrium. Through deliberate efforts to unplug, cultivate mindfulness, and nourish healthy relationships, we can reclaim our productivity, creativity, and emotional well-being.

As we embark on this quest for balance, let us remember that technology, at its core, is a tool - a means to enhance our lives and better the world. By adopting a balanced approach, we can harness its immense potential while preserving the essence of what makes us human. "The Tech Diet" offers a roadmap to navigate the digital landscape with wisdom, intention, and self-awareness, ultimately leading us towards a more fulfilling and harmonious coexistence with technology.

B. The Need for Balance: Recognizing the impact of tech overload on our lives

In the fast-paced, hyperconnected world we inhabit, technology has become an indispensable part of our daily lives. From smartphones that serve as pocket-sized computers to the myriad of apps and social media platforms at our fingertips, we are immersed in a digital ecosystem that offers unparalleled convenience and connectivity. However, amid this tech revolution, there is an underlying concern that demands our attention - the need for balance.

The impact of tech overload on our lives has become increasingly evident, shaping our behavior, relationships, and overall well-being. While technology has empowered us in countless ways, it has also introduced a range of challenges that require careful consideration.

One of the most significant consequences of tech overload is the decline of genuine human connection. As we become engrossed in our digital devices, engrossed in scrolling through feeds, or responding to messages, we may inadvertently neglect the meaningful face-to-face interactions that enrich our lives. The warmth of physical presence, the nuances of nonverbal communication, and the emotional depth of personal conversations can be overshadowed by the allure of virtual interactions.

Moreover, the constant exposure to a digital stream of information can lead to information overload. We are bombarded with an endless stream of news, notifications, emails, and updates that demand our immediate attention. As a result, we may struggle to filter and prioritize information, leading to decision fatigue and reduced cognitive capacity.

The addictive nature of technology is another pressing concern. App developers and tech companies employ sophisticated techniques to keep users engaged for extended periods. The result is a growing dependence on digital devices, often leading to excessive screen time that can negatively impact our physical and mental health. Sleep disturbances, eye strain, and decreased physical activity are just some of the consequences of excessive tech usage.

Tech overload can also take a toll on our productivity and creativity. The constant interruptions from notifications and the temptation to multitask can hinder our ability to concentrate deeply on tasks and foster innovative thinking. As a result, we may find ourselves trapped in a cycle of busyness, accomplishing shallow work instead of making meaningful progress.

Furthermore, the emotional implications of tech overload cannot be ignored. The relentless exposure to curated images of others' lives on social media can trigger feelings of inadequacy, envy, and anxiety. The pressure to maintain a perfect online persona can contribute to identity struggles and diminish our sense of authenticity.

Recognizing the need for balance is the first step towards reclaiming our agency over technology. As we delve into "The Tech Diet," we will explore various strategies to strike a harmonious equilibrium between the digital world and our real lives. It is not a call to abandon technology but rather a call to be mindful of its impact and to cultivate a conscious relationship with it.

By acknowledging the profound influence of tech overload on our lives, we empower ourselves to make informed choices and set healthy boundaries. We seek to find ways to use technology purposefully, to enhance our lives, foster meaningful connections, boost productivity, and promote mental and emotional well-being. The journey towards balance in a hyperconnected world begins with a deeper understanding of the impact of technology, and "The Tech Diet" offers the guidance we need to navigate this intricate terrain with wisdom and intention.

C. Introducing the Tech Diet: An approach to restoring equilibrium

In the midst of the digital age's whirlwind progress, where technology permeates every facet of our existence, we find ourselves confronted with a pressing need – the need to restore equilibrium in a hyperconnected world. This need has given birth to an innovative approach that seeks to address the challenges of tech overload and foster a harmonious coexistence with technology – The Tech Diet.

The Tech Diet is not your typical diet plan, aiming to restrict or eliminate certain aspects of our lives. Instead, it is a holistic and mindful approach to navigate the vast landscape of technology while maintaining a healthy balance. Much like a traditional diet, it emphasizes moderation, conscious consumption, and fostering habits that nourish our well-being.

The concept of a Tech Diet arises from the recognition that technology has become an integral part of modern society, shaping the way we interact, work, and perceive the world. However, the unbridled consumption of technology, often driven by habit and societal pressures, has led to unintended consequences. From the erosion of genuine human connection to the mental and emotional toll of constant comparison on social media, the imbalances caused by tech overload are becoming increasingly evident.

Introducing the Tech Diet entails embracing the art of digital mindfulness – a purposeful and deliberate approach to our tech usage. It encourages us to step back and assess how technology influences our lives, both positively and negatively. By gaining a deeper understanding of these influences, we can make informed decisions about our tech habits and curate a digital experience that aligns with our values and goals.

Central to the Tech Diet is the practice of unplugging to reconnect with ourselves and the world around us. This involves setting aside dedicated time to detach from screens and notifications, allowing us to be present and engaged in the richness of the present moment. Unplugging gives us space to rejuvenate, reflect, and appreciate the beauty of life beyond the digital realm.

Mindfulness, a pillar of the Tech Diet, empowers us to be aware of our tech usage and its impact on our well-being. By cultivating mindfulness, we can resist the allure of mindless scrolling and develop the ability to focus deeply on tasks, promoting greater productivity and creativity.

At the core of the Tech Diet is the belief that technology should serve as a tool to enhance our lives, not dominate them. It encourages us to adopt intentional tech usage, where we consciously choose how and when to engage with technology, aligning it with our goals and values.

The Tech Diet is also about nourishing healthy relationships – both online and offline. It calls for a thoughtful evaluation of the relationships we build through technology and emphasizes the importance of fostering genuine connections. By nurturing authentic interactions and empathy, we can create a digital landscape that promotes positivity and support rather than division and toxicity.

In the pages of "The Tech Diet: Finding Balance in a Hyperconnected World," we will explore practical strategies, research-backed insights, and inspiring stories to guide us on this transformative journey. The Tech Diet is not about cutting out technology completely; it is about finding a sustainable and enriching balance. By embracing the principles of the Tech Diet, we embark on a path to reclaim our agency over technology, restore equilibrium in our lives, and lead a fulfilling existence in this hyperconnected world.

CHAPTER II
Unplugging and Mindful Awareness

A. Disconnect to Reconnect: Embracing the Benefits of Digital Detox

In a world where constant connectivity is celebrated, the idea of disconnecting from our digital devices might seem counterintuitive. However, the benefits of a digital detox are profound, offering a refreshing perspective on life and a chance to reconnect with ourselves and the world around us.

Digital detox, often referred to as unplugging, involves intentionally stepping away from screens, social media, and digital distractions for a designated period. It is an opportunity to break free from the relentless stream of notifications, emails, and updates that monopolize our attention and time.

One of the primary advantages of a digital detox is the restoration of mental clarity. The constant bombardment of information and stimuli can overload our brains, leading to a phenomenon known as information overload. By unplugging, we give our minds a much-needed break, allowing them to recharge and process information more efficiently.

Moreover, a digital detox provides us with the space and time to reconnect with the present moment. We often find ourselves immersed in the virtual world, scrolling through social media feeds or responding to work emails even during moments that could be spent engaging with our immediate surroundings and loved ones. By disconnecting, we become more attuned to the world around us, appreciating the beauty of nature, the joys of face-to-face conversations, and the simple pleasures of life.

Unplugging can also lead to a reduction in stress and anxiety. The fear of missing out (FOMO) and the pressure to be constantly available through our devices can take a toll on our mental health. A digital detox liberates us from these anxieties, enabling us to live in the present and focus on self-care.

Furthermore, disconnecting from technology fosters the rekindling of creativity and introspection. In the absence of constant external stimuli, our minds are free to wander, imagine, and create. It is during these moments of silence and stillness that some of our most profound insights and ideas emerge.

Another significant advantage of a digital detox is improved sleep quality. The blue light emitted by screens can disrupt our sleep patterns and lead to sleep disturbances. By disconnecting before bedtime, we allow our bodies to naturally wind down, leading to more restful and rejuvenating sleep.

The benefits of unplugging extend beyond individual well-being. Families and friends who engage in digital detox together often report a strengthening of bonds and more meaningful interactions. By being fully present with one another, they create lasting memories and build stronger relationships.

Embracing the digital detox does not imply a complete rejection of technology; rather, it encourages us to use technology mindfully and purposefully. By incorporating regular digital detoxes into our lives, we can strike a healthier balance between our digital and real-world experiences.

In "The Tech Diet," we will explore practical tips and strategies to implement a digital detox successfully. From setting boundaries on tech usage to discovering alternative activities that enrich our lives, we will learn how to embrace the benefits of disconnecting, allowing us to reconnect with ourselves, our loved ones, and the wonders of the world that surround us.

B. Cultivating Mindfulness: Techniques to Regain Focus and Reduce Distractions

In the age of hyperconnectivity, cultivating mindfulness has become an essential skill to navigate the digital landscape and regain control over our attention. Mindfulness, at its core, is the practice of being fully present in the moment, aware of our thoughts, feelings, and surroundings without judgment. By developing this awareness, we can reclaim our focus, reduce distractions, and cultivate a more intentional and purposeful relationship with technology.

One powerful technique to foster mindfulness in a tech-dominated world is the practice of mindful breathing. Taking a few moments each day to focus on our breath can anchor us to the present and calm the incessant chatter of our minds. By paying attention to the inhalation and exhalation, we redirect our awareness away from digital distractions and center ourselves in the here and now.

Another effective way to cultivate mindfulness is through mindful technology usage. This involves approaching our devices with intention and presence rather than mindlessly engaging with them. Before reaching for our phones or computers, we can pause and ask ourselves why we are using them. By setting specific goals for our tech usage and being aware of our motives, we can avoid falling into the trap of aimless scrolling and time-wasting.

Mindful awareness also extends to our digital interactions and social media usage. When engaging with others online, we can practice empathy and compassion by recognizing that behind every profile is a real person with emotions and experiences. Avoiding toxic behavior and cultivating positive interactions not only benefit our well-being but also contribute to a healthier online environment for all.

Mindfulness can be further nurtured through the practice of single-tasking, a stark contrast to the prevalent habit of multitasking. Single-tasking involves giving our full attention to one activity at a time, allowing us to immerse ourselves deeply in the task at hand. By avoiding the constant switching of focus, we enhance our productivity and the quality of our work.

Mindful eating is another aspect of daily life that can positively impact our relationship with technology. By savoring our meals and fully engaging in the sensory experience of eating, we reduce the urge to mindlessly scroll through our phones while dining. This practice not only enhances our enjoyment of food but also promotes mindful living in all aspects of our day.

Practicing mindfulness may also involve designating specific tech-free zones or times in our daily routines. Creating sacred spaces where technology is prohibited allows us to disconnect from the digital world and fully immerse ourselves in real-world experiences. Similarly, designating tech-free hours before bedtime can improve sleep quality and contribute to a more restful and rejuvenating slumber.

"The Tech Diet" will delve into these mindfulness techniques and more, empowering readers to regain control over their attention and reduce the pervasive distractions of the digital age. By nurturing mindfulness, we can develop a greater sense of self-awareness and create a more intentional relationship with technology. With mindfulness as our ally, we can embrace the benefits of technology while maintaining balance and well-being in our hyperconnected lives.

CHAPTER III
Nourishing Healthy Relationships

A. The Social Media Conundrum: Balancing Virtual Connections with Real-Life Interactions

Social media has revolutionized the way we connect with others, breaking down geographical barriers and enabling us to stay in touch with friends, family, and acquaintances from around the world. It has undoubtedly enriched our social lives, but it has also given rise to a conundrum - the delicate balance between virtual connections and meaningful real-life interactions.

On one hand, social media provides us with an unprecedented opportunity to build and maintain relationships regardless of distance. We can share updates, photos, and videos, and engage in conversations with a wide network of people. These platforms foster a sense of belonging and community, especially for individuals who may feel isolated or marginalized in their physical surroundings.

However, the lure of virtual connections can overshadow the importance of face-to-face interactions. Spending excessive time on social media can lead to a phenomenon known as "social displacement," where online interactions displace real-life interactions. This can weaken the depth and quality of our relationships, as the nuances of in-person communication, such as tone of voice and body language, are lost in the digital realm.

Moreover, the curated nature of social media can create an illusion of superficiality. People tend to showcase their highlight reels, projecting an idealized version of their lives. This can lead to feelings of inadequacy and comparison, as we measure ourselves against the seemingly perfect lives of others. These feelings can erode our self-esteem and hinder genuine connections, as we fear not living up to the standards set by social media.

Finding the balance between virtual and real-life interactions is crucial for nurturing healthy relationships. It begins with self-awareness and understanding our motivations for using social media. By reflecting on our intentions, we can identify whether we are using these platforms as a tool for genuine connection or as a means of validation and escape.

Setting boundaries on social media usage is another key aspect of maintaining balance. Allocating specific time slots for checking social media and adhering to those boundaries can prevent the intrusion of virtual interactions into our personal and professional lives. This creates space for meaningful real-life connections without the constant distractions of digital notifications.

Furthermore, fostering genuine connections offline requires active effort and intention. Making time for face-to-face interactions with friends and loved ones allows us to cultivate deeper emotional bonds and create lasting memories. Engaging in activities together, such as shared hobbies, sports, or simply enjoying a meal, can strengthen the foundation of our relationships.

Embracing digital mindfulness during social interactions is essential. When spending time with others, being fully present and engaged without succumbing to the temptation of checking our phones can enhance the quality of our interactions. By giving our undivided attention to the people we are with, we show respect and appreciation for their presence in our lives.

"The Tech Diet" will explore practical strategies to strike a balance between virtual connections and real-life interactions. By navigating the social media conundrum with wisdom and intention, we can foster healthier relationships, strengthen our social connections, and create a sense of fulfillment in both our digital and physical worlds.

B. Fostering Empathy and Compassion: Navigating Technology's Influence on Human Relationships

As technology continues to shape the way we interact and communicate, fostering empathy and compassion in our digital age becomes both a challenge and a necessity. While social media and digital platforms have brought us closer in some ways, they have also introduced new complexities that can hinder our ability to connect with others on a deep emotional level.

One of the key challenges in the digital realm is the depersonalization of communication. Text-based interactions devoid of tone and facial expressions can lead to misinterpretations and misunderstandings. What may have been intended as a harmless comment might be misconstrued as hurtful or offensive, leading to unnecessary conflicts and emotional distress.

Moreover, the fast-paced nature of online conversations often encourages hasty responses, leaving little room for thoughtful consideration of others' feelings. The lack of immediate feedback in asynchronous communication can diminish our sense of responsibility for the impact of our words on others, contributing to the proliferation of online negativity and cyberbullying.

In navigating technology's influence on human relationships, it is vital to recognize that empathy and compassion lie at the heart of meaningful connections. Understanding and sharing the emotions of others can foster trust, strengthen bonds, and create a sense of belonging. Therefore, we must strive to cultivate these qualities in our digital interactions as much as in face-to-face encounters.

A crucial aspect of fostering empathy and compassion is active listening. In an era where information is readily available and attention spans are short, truly listening to others has become a rare and valuable skill. By giving our undivided attention to someone's thoughts and feelings, we validate their experiences and demonstrate that we care about their well-being.

Furthermore, practicing empathy online involves refraining from making assumptions about others based on limited information. Instead of jumping to conclusions or passing judgment, we can ask open-ended questions and seek to understand the context and emotions behind someone's statements. This willingness to see beyond surface-level interactions can lead to more meaningful and empathetic conversations.

In addition to cultivating empathy in our digital interactions, we can also use technology as a platform to spread compassion and kindness. Engaging in positive and uplifting conversations, supporting others in times of need, and promoting messages of understanding and empathy can create a ripple effect of compassion in the digital world.

To navigate technology's influence on human relationships effectively, it is essential to strike a balance between virtual interactions and face-to-face connections. While social media can serve as a conduit for initial connections, nurturing deeper relationships often requires the warmth and intimacy of in-person interactions.

"The Tech Diet" will delve into practical techniques for fostering empathy and compassion in a hyperconnected world. By embracing digital mindfulness and approaching technology with kindness, we can foster healthier and more fulfilling relationships both online and offline. Empathy and compassion are the cornerstones of a thriving social landscape, and by prioritizing these qualities, we can navigate the complexities of technology and build meaningful connections that enrich our lives and the lives of others.

CHAPTER IV
Reclaiming Productivity and Creativity

A. The Myth of Multitasking: Exploring the Pitfalls and Benefits of Task-Switching

In our fast-paced and technology-driven world, multitasking has become a badge of honor, symbolizing efficiency and productivity. We often find ourselves juggling multiple tasks simultaneously, believing that we are making the most of our time. However, beneath this perception lies the myth of multitasking - the belief that we can effectively focus on multiple tasks at once without compromising our performance. In reality, task-switching, often mistaken for multitasking, comes with its pitfalls and benefits that deserve a closer examination.

The common misconception is that multitasking enhances productivity, allowing us to accomplish more in less time. However, research has consistently shown that the human brain is not designed for true multitasking. Rather than handling multiple tasks simultaneously, our brain rapidly switches attention between them. This constant shifting of focus creates what psychologists call "switching costs," where time and mental resources are wasted in the process of transitioning from one task to another.

One of the primary pitfalls of task-switching is a decrease in overall efficiency and accuracy. Studies reveal that when we switch between tasks, our performance suffers, and errors increase. We become more prone to overlook details, make mistakes, and experience mental fatigue due to the cognitive strain of constant switching.

Moreover, multitasking can negatively impact our ability to concentrate deeply on tasks. In a world where distractions abound, the habit of task-switching can further erode our attention spans and make it challenging to engage in focused, uninterrupted work - a state known as "deep work," which is essential for creativity and problem-solving.

Furthermore, the constant buzz of notifications and the dopamine rush of switching tasks can create an addiction-like cycle, making it difficult to resist the urge to multitask. This addiction to the quick rewards of task-switching can hinder our capacity for sustained concentration and prevent us from delving deeply into complex projects that require extended periods of attention.

However, task-switching does have some benefits, especially in specific contexts. In certain professions, such as emergency response or critical decision-making scenarios, the ability to shift attention rapidly between tasks can be crucial. Additionally, for repetitive or mundane tasks, alternating between them can help break the monotony and maintain focus.

Recognizing the myth of multitasking allows us to reclaim our productivity and creativity. Embracing the concept of "unitasking" or focusing on one task at a time can lead to better outcomes and a sense of accomplishment. By dedicating our attention fully to each task, we can perform more efficiently and produce higher-quality work.

To combat the allure of task-switching, we can implement strategies such as time blocking, where we allocate specific periods for focused work on individual tasks. Setting clear priorities and eliminating distractions during these periods can help us maintain concentration and achieve better results.

In "The Tech Diet," we will explore techniques to reclaim productivity and creativity by debunking the myth of multitasking. By understanding the pitfalls of task-switching and adopting a mindful approach to work, we can optimize our performance, foster creativity, and lead a more fulfilling and balanced professional life.

B. Rediscovering Deep Work: Techniques to Boost Productivity and Unleash Creativity

In our technology-driven world, the constant barrage of distractions and the allure of instant gratification have taken a toll on our ability to engage in deep, focused work. Deep work, a concept popularized by productivity expert Cal Newport, refers to the state of flow where we immerse ourselves in meaningful, undistracted work, leading to heightened productivity and creativity. As we seek to reclaim our productivity and unleash our creative potential, it is essential to rediscover the art of deep work.

One of the foundational techniques to cultivate deep work is the establishment of a distraction-free environment. By minimizing interruptions from digital devices, notifications, and social media, we create a space conducive to focused attention. This may involve setting specific times for checking emails and messages or utilizing website blockers to limit access to distracting websites during work sessions.

Time blocking is another powerful technique to prioritize deep work. By scheduling dedicated blocks of time for focused work on specific tasks, we create a rhythm that allows us to delve deeply into projects without interruptions. This structured approach helps us make progress on complex tasks and prevents procrastination.

Another aspect of rediscovering deep work is setting clear goals and intentions for each work session.

Knowing what needs to be accomplished and having a clear plan of action enhances our focus and minimizes time spent on unnecessary distractions. Goal-setting also provides a sense of purpose and direction, boosting motivation and productivity.

Incorporating periods of rest and renewal is essential for sustaining deep work over time. The brain requires time to recharge and process information. Therefore, interspersing deep work sessions with short breaks can improve cognitive function and prevent burnout. Engaging in activities such as meditation, exercise, or spending time in nature during breaks can also enhance creativity and mental clarity.

Embracing the art of monotasking, or single-tasking, is fundamental to deep work. Contrary to the prevalent habit of multitasking, monotasking involves giving our full attention to one task at a time. This level of immersion allows us to perform at our peak and achieve higher-quality outcomes.

Moreover, establishing a routine or ritual before engaging in deep work can help signal the brain that it is time to focus. Simple actions like lighting a candle, listening to calming music, or practicing a brief mindfulness exercise can serve as triggers to enter a state of deep concentration.

Furthermore, embracing deep work requires training the mind to resist the allure of distraction. By practicing mindfulness and cultivating self-awareness, we can catch ourselves when our attention begins to drift and gently redirect it back to the task at hand.

In "The Tech Diet," we will delve into these techniques and more to rediscover the art of deep work and unleash our full productivity and creativity potential. By fostering a distraction-free environment, setting clear intentions, and integrating periods of rest and renewal, we can tap into the depths of our minds and achieve meaningful, impactful work. Rediscovering the joy of deep work is not only a path to reclaiming our productivity but also a gateway to unlocking the boundless realms of our creative genius.

CHAPTER V
Mental and Emotional Well-being

A. Addressing Technostress: Recognizing and Managing the Psychological Toll of Technology

In our hyperconnected world, technology has become an integral part of our daily lives, transforming the way we work, communicate, and live. While technology offers numerous benefits and conveniences, it also brings with it a psychological toll known as technostress. Addressing this growing concern is crucial for safeguarding our mental and emotional well-being in the digital age.

Technostress refers to the stress and negative psychological effects that arise from our interactions with technology. It can manifest in various ways, such as anxiety, burnout, and a sense of being overwhelmed by the constant demands of digital devices and online communication.

One of the primary sources of technostress is the constant connectivity that technology affords. The expectation to be reachable 24/7, both personally and professionally, can create a sense of pressure and anxiety, leaving us feeling trapped in a perpetual cycle of digital responsiveness.

Moreover, the never-ending stream of information and notifications can lead to information overload, where we struggle to filter and process the vast amount of data available to us. This cognitive overload can diminish our ability to focus, make decisions, and maintain a sense of clarity.

The addictive nature of technology is another contributing factor to technostress. The pull of social media, online entertainment, and compulsive email checking can consume large chunks of our time, leaving us feeling disconnected from reality and our own emotions.

Furthermore, the phenomenon of "compare and despair" on social media can exacerbate feelings of inadequacy and discontent. Constantly comparing ourselves to carefully curated images and experiences shared by others can lead to a distorted perception of reality and breed feelings of envy and self-doubt.

Addressing technostress begins with recognizing the signs and acknowledging its impact on our well-being. Being mindful of our emotional responses to technology and paying attention to how much time we spend online can help us identify potential sources of technostress in our lives.

Setting healthy boundaries with technology is a key strategy for managing technostress. Establishing designated tech-free times or creating digital detox periods can provide much-needed respite from the constant connectivity. Prioritizing face-to-face interactions and engaging in activities that promote relaxation and stress reduction can also be beneficial in managing technostress.

Practicing digital mindfulness is another essential component of addressing technostress. Being intentional and purposeful in our tech usage, and taking regular breaks from screens, can help us regain control over our technology habits and reduce the negative impact on our mental well-being.

In "The Tech Diet," we will delve into effective techniques and coping mechanisms to address technostress and protect our mental and emotional well-being. By fostering a healthy relationship with technology and cultivating digital resilience, we can navigate the digital landscape with greater ease and balance, promoting a sense of peace and harmony amidst the demands of the modern world.

B. Cultivating Digital Mindfulness: Strategies to Protect Mental Health in a Hyperconnected World

In the age of hyperconnectivity, cultivating digital mindfulness has become an essential practice to safeguard our mental and emotional well-being. Digital mindfulness refers to the intentional and conscious use of technology, where we strive to strike a harmonious balance between our digital and real-world experiences. By adopting strategies to protect our mental health in a hyperconnected world, we can navigate the digital landscape with greater resilience and self-awareness.

One of the fundamental principles of digital mindfulness is setting clear boundaries on our technology usage. By establishing specific times for engaging with digital devices and designating tech-free zones, we create spaces in our lives where we can disconnect and be fully present in the moment. This practice allows us to reclaim our attention and prevents technology from becoming an omnipresent force that disrupts our mental and emotional well-being.

Creating a mindful morning routine can set the tone for the rest of the day. Instead of immediately reaching for our phones upon waking, we can engage in activities that promote well-being, such as meditation, journaling, or simply enjoying a quiet moment with a cup of tea. This intentional start to the day helps us establish a positive and focused mindset before being bombarded by external digital stimuli.

Mindful digital consumption involves being discerning about the content we engage with online. Curating our digital feeds to include positive and inspiring content can contribute to a more uplifting and nourishing online experience. Unfollowing accounts that trigger negative emotions or induce feelings of inadequacy can protect our mental health and promote a sense of self-empowerment.

Furthermore, adopting the "one screen at a time" rule can reduce the cognitive load and prevent information overload. By limiting our attention to one digital task or app, we avoid the overwhelming feeling of multitasking and allow ourselves to focus more deeply on the present moment.

Practicing gratitude in the digital realm can also contribute to our mental well-being. Amidst the constant pursuit of more content, connections, and achievements, taking a moment to express gratitude for the blessings we already have can shift our perspective and foster contentment.

Engaging in digital detox periods is a crucial aspect of digital mindfulness. Scheduling regular breaks from screens, whether for a few hours, a day, or longer, allows us to recharge and refresh our minds. During these detox periods, we can embrace activities that nourish our mental health, such as spending time in nature, reading a book, or engaging in creative hobbies.

In "The Tech Diet," we will explore a plethora of practical strategies to cultivate digital mindfulness and protect our mental health in a hyperconnected world. By adopting these techniques and embracing a purposeful approach to technology, we can navigate the digital landscape with wisdom and intention, ultimately leading to a more balanced, fulfilling, and emotionally resilient existence. Cultivating digital mindfulness is not about shunning technology but rather about reclaiming our agency over it and using it as a tool to enhance our lives and well-being.

CHAPTER VI
Raising Tech-Savvy and Balanced Children

A. Parenting in the Digital Age: Navigating the Challenges of Raising Tech-Conscious Kids

As technology continues to shape the world, parenting in the digital age presents a unique set of challenges and responsibilities. While digital devices and the internet offer countless opportunities for learning and connection, they also bring concerns about screen time, online safety, and the impact of technology on children's development. Navigating these challenges requires a balanced approach that cultivates tech-savviness while nurturing emotional well-being.

One of the primary concerns in the digital age is managing children's screen time. The allure of digital entertainment can easily lead to excessive device use, which may have adverse effects on children's sleep, physical health, and social skills. Setting age-appropriate limits on screen time and creating tech-free zones in the home can establish healthy boundaries and encourage children to engage in other enriching activities.

Online safety is another crucial aspect of parenting in the digital age. Teaching children about internet safety, privacy, and responsible online behavior is essential to protect them from potential risks and dangers online. Open communication and fostering a trusting relationship with children enable them to feel comfortable seeking guidance and support when navigating the digital world.

Balancing virtual interactions with face-to-face connections is key to promoting social skills and emotional intelligence in children. Encouraging real-life play, outdoor activities, and quality family time helps children develop meaningful connections and emotional bonds. Parents can also model healthy tech habits by being mindful of their own tech usage and demonstrating the importance of being fully present in offline interactions.

Educating children about media literacy and critical thinking is essential in an era of information overload. Teaching them how to discern credible sources from misinformation and propaganda empowers them to be informed and responsible digital citizens. Encouraging active engagement with educational content and creative platforms can harness technology as a tool for learning and self-expression.

Emphasizing the value of face-to-face communication and active listening helps children develop empathy and emotional intelligence. Engaging in regular family discussions and providing a safe space for children to express their thoughts and feelings fosters a sense of emotional well-being and connectivity in the family unit.

Parental involvement and supervision play a crucial role in nurturing tech-conscious kids. Installing parental controls and monitoring online activities can help ensure children's safety while they explore the digital realm. However, striking a balance between supervision and granting age-appropriate independence is essential to foster a sense of trust and autonomy in children.

In "The Tech Diet," we will explore strategies and insights to guide parents in raising tech-savvy and balanced children. By embracing a mindful and informed approach to parenting in the digital age, we can equip our children with the skills they need to thrive in a technology-driven world while nurturing their emotional well-being and promoting meaningful real-world connections. Parenting in the digital age requires adaptability, understanding, and an unwavering commitment to fostering a healthy relationship between children and technology.

B. Creating Tech Rules: Instilling Responsible Digital Habits in Children

In a rapidly advancing digital landscape, creating tech rules is a fundamental aspect of parenting to instill responsible digital habits in children. As technology becomes an integral part of their lives, establishing clear guidelines for tech usage is essential to ensure a balanced and healthy relationship with digital devices. By fostering responsible digital habits from an early age, parents can empower their children to navigate the digital world safely and responsibly.

Setting age-appropriate limits on screen time is a crucial starting point for creating tech rules. Different age groups have varying developmental needs and tolerance for technology. Younger children may require more supervised and restricted screen time, while older children can handle more independence. By considering age and individual circumstances, parents can strike a balance between allowing digital exploration and protecting their children from excessive screen exposure.

Creating tech-free zones and times in the household is an effective way to promote face-to-face interactions and family bonding. Designating mealtime, family outings, and bedtime as tech-free periods encourages children to be present and engaged in real-life interactions. It also helps prevent the intrusion of technology into essential family moments.

Establishing rules for responsible online behavior is vital in cultivating good digital citizenship. Children should be taught to respect others' privacy, refrain from cyberbullying, and think critically before sharing personal information online. Emphasizing the impact of their digital actions on others helps children understand the importance of responsible digital conduct.

Educating children about the potential risks and dangers of the internet is essential for their safety. Parents can teach their children to identify and avoid harmful content, malicious websites, and online scams. Open conversations about online safety and the importance of seeking help if they encounter any concerning situations empower children to protect themselves while exploring the digital world.

Modeling responsible tech usage is a powerful way for parents to lead by example. Children often mirror their parents' behavior, so demonstrating mindful tech habits and setting boundaries for personal tech usage can leave a lasting impression on children. When parents prioritize face-to-face interactions, practice digital detox, and engage in meaningful offline activities, children are more likely to follow suit.

Encouraging a balance of tech time with other activities, such as physical play, reading, and creative hobbies, fosters well-rounded development. Parents can create a daily schedule that includes a mix of tech-related and non-tech-related activities, allowing children to explore their interests while promoting a balanced lifestyle.

In "The Tech Diet," we will delve into practical strategies for creating tech rules and instilling responsible digital habits in children. By nurturing a mindful and informed approach to tech usage, parents can empower their children to become tech-savvy and responsible digital citizens. The goal is not to restrict technology but rather to use it as a valuable tool while promoting essential values and skills that contribute to a balanced and fulfilling life in the digital age.

CHAPTER VII
Designing a Healthy Digital Lifestyle

A. Leveraging Technology for Good: Utilizing Apps and Tools to Enhance Well-being

In our tech-dominated world, the idea of a healthy digital lifestyle might seem elusive. However, when used mindfully, technology can be a powerful ally in promoting overall well-being and enriching our lives. Embracing the concept of leveraging technology for good involves being intentional about the apps and tools we incorporate into our daily routines, choosing those that support our physical, mental, and emotional health.

Fitness and wellness apps have revolutionized the way we approach health and self-care. With a plethora of apps available, individuals can personalize their fitness routines, monitor their progress, and set achievable goals. These apps provide guided workouts, meditation sessions, sleep tracking, and nutrition planning, empowering users to take charge of their well-being in a way that fits their unique needs and preferences.

Mindfulness and meditation apps offer a respite from the fast-paced digital world, allowing users to cultivate inner calm and self-awareness. These apps provide guided meditation sessions, breathing exercises, and stress-relief techniques, facilitating mindfulness practices that can reduce anxiety, improve focus, and foster emotional resilience.

Digital journaling tools have transformed the way we express our thoughts and emotions. Journaling apps provide a private and secure space to document daily reflections, set intentions, and explore personal growth. The act of journaling can serve as a therapeutic outlet for emotions and a means of processing life's challenges, promoting mental clarity and emotional well-being.

Sleep tracking apps have gained popularity as individuals seek to optimize their sleep patterns for better health. By monitoring sleep quality, duration, and habits, users can identify factors that may be affecting their sleep and make adjustments to improve overall restfulness and daytime alertness.

Language learning apps enable users to expand their horizons and connect with other cultures. Learning a new language not only enhances cognitive abilities but also fosters a sense of cultural understanding and empathy.

Gratitude and positivity apps encourage a focus on gratitude and optimism. These apps prompt users to record daily moments of gratitude and positive affirmations, fostering a mindset of appreciation and abundance.

Moreover, time management and productivity apps help users stay organized, prioritize tasks, and avoid digital distractions. These tools can enhance productivity and free up time for other fulfilling activities.

It is important to be mindful of the potential drawbacks of technology and avoid excessive reliance on digital devices. The goal is to integrate technology as a tool that complements our lives rather than dominates them.

In "The Tech Diet," we will explore a diverse range of apps and tools that can enhance well-being and contribute to a healthy digital lifestyle. By harnessing technology mindfully and with intention, we can leverage its benefits to cultivate a more balanced, fulfilling, and joyful life in our ever-evolving digital world.

B. Setting Boundaries: Establishing Healthy Tech Usage Habits for a Balanced Life

In our technology-driven era, setting boundaries around tech usage is essential for designing a healthy digital lifestyle. The pervasive presence of digital devices and the constant stream of information can easily lead to a sense of overwhelm and imbalance. By establishing healthy tech habits and boundaries, we can regain control over our digital lives and create space for meaningful real-world experiences.

One of the first steps in setting boundaries is conducting a digital audit. Reflecting on our tech usage patterns allows us to identify areas where we may be spending excessive time or engaging in mindless scrolling. This self-awareness provides a foundation for creating personalized boundaries that address our unique needs and challenges.

Creating a tech schedule is an effective strategy to manage digital time wisely. Allocating specific time slots for checking emails, social media, and other digital tasks prevents technology from encroaching on other aspects of our lives. This conscious approach to tech usage promotes focused work, prevents distractions, and frees up time for other meaningful activities.

Establishing tech-free zones in the home encourages present-moment living and fosters better communication among family members. Designating spaces, such as the dining area or bedrooms, as tech-free zones promotes face-to-face interactions and ensures that digital devices do not interfere with quality family time.

A bedtime tech curfew can significantly impact sleep quality and overall well-being. The blue light emitted by screens can disrupt circadian rhythms and hinder the body's ability to wind down before sleep. By setting a curfew for technology use an hour before bedtime, we create a buffer zone that allows us to relax and prepare for a restful night's sleep.

Setting boundaries around notifications is vital for minimizing distractions and maintaining focus. Disabling non-essential notifications during work hours or designated focus periods reduces the temptation to check our phones constantly and allows us to concentrate on tasks with greater depth and efficiency.

Practicing digital detoxes or screen-free days on a regular basis is a rejuvenating way to reset and recharge. Digital detoxes involve consciously unplugging from screens and social media for a set period, allowing us to connect with ourselves and the world around us without digital interference.

Educating family members about the importance of setting boundaries and modeling responsible tech habits is essential, especially in households with children. By leading by example, parents can instill healthy tech usage habits in their children and create an environment that prioritizes human connection and well-being over digital distractions.

In "The Tech Diet," we will explore practical tips and techniques for setting boundaries and establishing healthy tech usage habits. By consciously integrating technology into our lives and being mindful of its impact, we can create a balanced digital lifestyle that supports our well-being, enhances our productivity, and fosters meaningful connections with others. Setting boundaries empowers us to embrace technology as a valuable tool while remaining in control of its influence in our lives.

CHAPTER VIII
The Future of Hyperconnectivity

A. Embracing Technological Advancements: Examining Potential Benefits and Risks

As hyperconnectivity continues to shape the trajectory of human progress, embracing technological advancements has become inevitable. The future promises a world that is even more interconnected, with transformative technologies permeating every aspect of our lives. However, as we move toward this future, it is essential to examine both the potential benefits and risks that come hand in hand with these advancements.

One of the most promising benefits of technological advancements is the potential for increased efficiency and productivity. Automation, artificial intelligence, and advanced data analytics are reshaping industries, streamlining processes, and optimizing decision-making. These advancements hold the promise of freeing up human resources to focus on more creative and value-driven tasks.

Furthermore, hyperconnectivity enables seamless communication and collaboration across borders, fostering a global community. The exchange of ideas, knowledge, and cultural experiences has never been more accessible, leading to unprecedented opportunities for cross-cultural understanding and cooperation.

In the healthcare sector, technological advancements offer the potential for transformative breakthroughs. Precision medicine, telemedicine, and wearable health devices are revolutionizing healthcare delivery and empowering individuals to take greater control of their well-being.

Education is also undergoing a significant transformation as technology becomes an integral part of the learning process. Online learning platforms, virtual classrooms, and personalized educational content are leveling the playing field and making quality education accessible to learners worldwide.

Moreover, technological advancements play a vital role in addressing environmental challenges. Green technologies, renewable energy solutions, and IoT-based environmental monitoring systems are helping to mitigate the impact of human activities on the planet and promote sustainability.

Despite the promising benefits, there are also risks associated with the future of hyperconnectivity. One of the primary concerns is the potential for increased cyber threats and data breaches. As technology permeates every aspect of our lives, the risk of cyberattacks on critical infrastructure, personal data, and national security becomes more pronounced.

Moreover, the increasing reliance on automation and AI raises questions about job displacement and economic inequality. The automation of certain tasks could lead to job loss in certain sectors, creating a need for reskilling and upskilling to ensure a smooth transition into new roles.

Privacy concerns are also at the forefront as hyperconnectivity gathers momentum. The extensive collection of personal data and the lack of robust data protection measures can lead to breaches of privacy and potential misuse of sensitive information.

Additionally, the rapid pace of technological advancements may outstrip the ability of regulatory frameworks to keep up. This creates challenges in ensuring ethical and responsible use of emerging technologies.

In "The Tech Diet," we will explore the future of hyperconnectivity and examine the potential benefits and risks. By embracing technological advancements mindfully and proactively addressing associated risks, we can shape a future where technology serves as a force for good, enhancing human lives and fostering a more equitable and sustainable world. Balancing innovation with responsibility will be key to navigating the exciting and ever-evolving landscape of hyperconnectivity.

B. Ethical Considerations: Balancing Innovation with Societal Well-being

As we venture into the future of hyperconnectivity, ethical considerations become paramount in navigating the complex interplay between technology and societal well-being. The rapid pace of technological advancements brings forth exciting opportunities, but it also raises significant ethical questions about how we use and integrate these innovations into our lives. Striking a balance between innovation and the well-being of individuals and communities is essential to harnessing the full potential of hyperconnectivity responsibly.

One of the key ethical considerations is data privacy and security. The vast amount of personal data collected and shared in a hyperconnected world demands stringent data protection measures. It is crucial for companies and governments to uphold the privacy rights of individuals and ensure that data is not misused or sold without consent. Strong data protection laws and transparent data practices are essential to building trust between users and technology providers.

Another ethical concern revolves around the increasing use of artificial intelligence (AI) and machine learning. As AI becomes more pervasive in various industries, questions arise about accountability, transparency, and potential biases in AI algorithms. Ensuring that AI systems are designed ethically and trained on diverse and representative datasets is vital to avoiding discriminatory outcomes and promoting fairness.

The potential for job displacement due to automation is another ethical dilemma. As technology advances and certain tasks become automated, there is a responsibility to address the impact on the workforce. Governments and organizations must proactively invest in reskilling and upskilling initiatives to support workers in transitioning to new roles and industries.

Furthermore, the ethical implications of hyperconnectivity extend to global disparities. While technological innovations can benefit many, there is a risk of leaving behind those without access to advanced technologies or the necessary digital literacy. Bridging the digital divide and ensuring equitable access to technology and digital education is crucial in creating an inclusive and just society.

The influence of technology on human behavior and mental health raises ethical questions about the design of digital platforms. Social media and other online services are engineered to capture and retain users' attention, often leading to addictive behaviors and negative psychological effects. Ethical design principles should prioritize user well-being and mental health over maximizing engagement and screen time.

In addition to individual well-being, hyperconnectivity has broader societal implications. The spread of misinformation, echo chambers, and algorithmic manipulation on social media platforms can undermine democratic processes and social cohesion. Ethical considerations demand a commitment to countering disinformation and promoting informed, unbiased, and diverse perspectives.

In "The Tech Diet," we will delve into ethical considerations in a hyperconnected world and explore strategies for responsibly integrating technology into society. By adopting ethical frameworks that prioritize the well-being of individuals, communities, and the environment, we can navigate the future of hyperconnectivity with integrity and ensure that technology serves as a force for positive change. Balancing innovation with ethical considerations is essential to shaping a future where technology benefits all of humanity and fosters a more sustainable and harmonious world.

CHAPTER IX
A Tech Diet for Life

A. Sustaining the Balance: Tips for Long-Term Adherence to the Tech Diet

Adopting a Tech Diet can be a transformative journey toward finding balance in a hyperconnected world. However, sustaining this balanced lifestyle over the long term requires commitment, mindfulness, and adaptability. As we strive to integrate technology in a way that enhances our lives rather than overwhelms them, these tips can serve as guiding principles for maintaining the Tech Diet for life.

❖ Set Realistic Goals: Start by setting achievable goals that align with your values and lifestyle. Be clear about why you want to follow the Tech Diet and what specific changes you hope to make. Setting realistic expectations ensures that you stay motivated and committed to the process.

❖ Practice Mindful Tech Usage: Be intentional about how you use technology. Practice digital mindfulness by regularly evaluating your tech habits and being aware of how they impact your well-being. Avoid mindless scrolling and instead use technology with purpose and focus.

❖ Establish Tech-Free Zones and Times: Designate specific areas or times in your daily routine where technology is off-limits. Create tech-free zones in your home, such as the bedroom, dining area, or family gathering spaces, to foster meaningful face-to-face interactions.

❖ Create a Tech Schedule: Develop a structured tech schedule that allows you to allocate time for different digital tasks. Set aside dedicated periods for work-related tech usage, social media, and leisure activities. This approach helps you strike a balance and prevents tech from encroaching on other aspects of your life.

❖ Prioritize Real-Life Connections: Foster meaningful relationships by prioritizing in-person interactions over virtual ones. Make time for quality face-to-face conversations, shared activities, and family bonding without the interference of technology.

❖ Regular Digital Detoxes: Plan regular digital detoxes to recharge and rejuvenate. During these detox periods, disconnect from screens and immerse yourself in offline activities that nourish your mind, body, and soul.

❖ Limit Notifications and Distractions: Disable non-essential notifications to minimize distractions. Set boundaries to prevent technology from interrupting your focus during important tasks or moments of relaxation.

❖ Practice Gratitude and Contentment: Cultivate a mindset of gratitude and contentment. Focus on what you have rather than what you lack, and avoid falling into the comparison trap facilitated by social media.

❖ Continuous Learning: Stay informed about the latest tech trends and how they may impact your life. Engage in continuous learning to understand the evolving digital landscape and make informed decisions about your tech usage.

❖ Be Kind to Yourself: Embrace the Tech Diet as a journey, not a destination. There will be times when you may slip back into old tech habits, and that's okay. Be kind to yourself, acknowledge your progress, and use any setbacks as opportunities to reassess and readjust your approach.

In "The Tech Diet," we emphasize the importance of viewing technology as a tool rather than a master. By following these tips and staying committed to the principles of the Tech Diet, you can sustain a balanced and mindful relationship with technology for the long term. The goal is to create a harmonious coexistence between technology and well-being, empowering you to lead a fulfilling and purpose-driven life in the hyperconnected world.

B. Empowering Others: Advocating for a Balanced and Mindful Tech Culture

As we embark on our own Tech Diet journey, we have the power to inspire and empower others to embrace a balanced and mindful tech culture. Advocating for responsible tech usage not only benefits individuals but also contributes to creating a healthier and more harmonious digital society. Here are some ways we can make a positive impact and become advocates for a Tech Diet lifestyle:

❖ Lead by Example: Be a role model for others by demonstrating the benefits of a Tech Diet in your own life. Share your experiences, successes, and challenges with others to inspire them to consider their own tech habits and make positive changes.

❖ Educate and Raise Awareness: Spread awareness about the importance of a balanced tech lifestyle through conversations, social media, and community events. Educate others about the potential impact of technology on mental health, well-being, and relationships.

❖ Promote Digital Literacy: Advocate for digital literacy programs in schools and communities to ensure that everyone has the knowledge and skills to navigate the digital world safely and responsibly.

❖ Engage in Tech Talks and Workshops: Organize or participate in workshops, seminars, or tech talks that focus on responsible tech usage and the benefits of a Tech Diet. Collaborate with experts, educators, and community leaders to create meaningful discussions.

❖ Support Digital Well-being Initiatives: Support and promote initiatives that prioritize digital well-being and mental health. Encourage the development of apps and technologies that enhance well-being rather than exploit attention.

❖ Encourage Mindful Tech Usage at Work: Advocate for mindful tech usage in the workplace to improve productivity and work-life balance. Suggest incorporating tech breaks, mindfulness practices, and digital detox challenges in the workplace culture.

❖ Involve Schools and Parents: Collaborate with schools and parents to create a holistic approach to tech education for children. Encourage open dialogues about responsible tech usage and digital citizenship.

❖ Partner with Tech Companies: Engage with tech companies and advocate for user-friendly features that promote digital well-being, such as screen time trackers, notification settings, and personalized content curation.

❖ Initiate Tech-Free Events: Organize or participate in tech-free events that encourage real-world connections and foster a sense of community without constant digital distractions.

❖ Be Empathetic and Non-Judgmental: Understand that everyone's journey with technology is unique. Be empathetic and non-judgmental, supporting others in finding a Tech Diet that works best for them.

By advocating for a balanced and mindful tech culture, we contribute to a more conscious and compassionate digital world. Our efforts to empower others can create a ripple effect, inspiring a generation of individuals who are aware of their tech habits and the impact of technology on their lives. Together, we can foster a tech culture that prioritizes human connection, well-being, and genuine fulfillment in the hyperconnected world. The Tech Diet is not just a personal journey—it's a collective movement towards a healthier and more harmonious tech ecosystem.

Conclusion

A. Embracing the Journey: Reflecting on Personal Growth and Transformation

As we conclude our journey through "The Tech Diet: Finding Balance in a Hyperconnected World," it is essential to reflect on the personal growth and transformation that comes with embracing a mindful and balanced tech lifestyle. Throughout this exploration, we have delved into the blessings and curses of hyperconnectivity, recognized the impact of tech overload on our lives, and discovered an approach to restore equilibrium—the Tech Diet.

By embracing the Tech Diet, we have learned to disconnect to reconnect, cultivating mindful awareness and reducing digital distractions. We have explored the conundrum of social media, learning to balance virtual connections with meaningful real-life interactions. Navigating technology's influence on human relationships, we have fostered empathy and compassion in a digital world. Understanding the pitfalls of multitasking, we have reclaimed productivity and unleashed our creativity through deep work techniques.

We have addressed the psychological toll of technology and taken steps to protect our mental and emotional well-being through digital mindfulness. In raising tech-savvy and balanced children, we have navigated the challenges of parenting in the digital age, instilling responsible tech habits and creating tech rules for their future well-being.

In designing a healthy digital lifestyle, we have leveraged technology for good, utilizing apps and tools to enhance our overall well-being. Ethical considerations have guided our journey, as we balance innovation with societal well-being, promoting an inclusive and sustainable digital world.

As we move forward, sustaining the Tech Diet requires commitment and self-awareness. We have set realistic goals and established boundaries that prioritize real-life connections and promote digital detoxes. By fostering a mindset of gratitude and contentment, we have embraced a more purposeful and fulfilling relationship with technology.

Our journey does not end here, for we have the power to empower others and advocate for a balanced and mindful tech culture. Through education, awareness, and empathy, we can inspire a generation of individuals who recognize the potential and risks of technology and choose to use it responsibly and consciously.

Embracing the Tech Diet has been transformative—a journey of personal growth, self-discovery, and empowerment. We have unlocked the potential to navigate the digital world with wisdom, intention, and compassion. In a hyperconnected world, we can forge a path toward balance, embracing technology as a tool that enhances our lives and nurtures our well-being.

As we continue this journey, let us remember that the Tech Diet is not a destination but an ongoing commitment to a balanced and mindful relationship with technology. Together, we can shape a future where humanity and technology coexist in harmony, creating a world where the true essence of human connection and fulfillment thrives amidst the wonders of the digital age. Embrace the journey of the Tech Diet and unlock the limitless possibilities that a balanced and mindful tech lifestyle can offer.

B. A Balanced Future: Envisioning a World Where Tech and Well-being Coexist Harmoniously

As we conclude our exploration of "The Tech Diet: Finding Balance in a Hyperconnected World," we envision a future where technology and well-being coexist in harmony—a world where hyperconnectivity enhances human lives rather than overshadowing them. Throughout this journey, we have discovered the blessings and curses of technology, recognized the need for balance in a hyperconnected world, and embraced the Tech Diet as a means to restore equilibrium.

In this balanced future, individuals have cultivated a mindful and intentional approach to technology. They have learned to disconnect from constant digital stimuli to reconnect with themselves and their surroundings. People prioritize real-life connections, cherishing face-to-face interactions, and meaningful relationships. They have developed the ability to navigate the digital realm responsibly, leveraging technology for personal growth, learning, and productivity.

Children grow up with a healthy relationship with technology, supported by parents who are tech-savvy and mindful. Families have tech-free zones and times, ensuring that precious moments are shared without distractions, fostering deep bonds and emotional connection. Children are equipped with digital literacy skills, ensuring that they navigate the online world safely and responsibly.

In this future, technology companies have evolved to prioritize user well-being over maximizing engagement and screen time. Ethical design principles are integrated into digital platforms, promoting positive user experiences and minimizing addictive elements. The focus is on delivering technology that enhances human potential and promotes genuine connection.

Education embraces the power of technology to enrich learning experiences. Schools offer a balanced curriculum that blends digital resources with real-world experiences. Digital literacy is a core component of education, empowering students to be responsible digital citizens and critical thinkers in the digital age.

The workplace of the future encourages a healthy work-life balance, with tech breaks and digital detox initiatives. Employers recognize that productivity is enhanced when employees are mentally and emotionally well. Mindful tech usage leads to increased creativity, focus, and overall job satisfaction.

In this balanced future, individuals and communities are actively engaged in promoting digital well-being. They advocate for responsible tech usage, organizing tech-free events, and supporting initiatives that prioritize mental health and digital literacy. The digital world becomes a space for meaningful connections and positive change.

Embracing the Tech Diet has sparked a transformative shift in how society views and interacts with technology.

It has paved the way for a balanced and harmonious future, where technology serves as a powerful tool for progress and connectivity without compromising our well-being.

As we envision this future, let us remember that each one of us plays a vital role in shaping it. By advocating for responsible tech usage and embracing a mindful approach to technology, we can collectively create a world where human values are at the core of technological advancements.

The journey of the Tech Diet is ongoing, and its impact will continue to grow as more individuals join this movement. Embrace the lessons learned and the principles of the Tech Diet, for they hold the potential to empower us and future generations to lead fulfilling and purpose-driven lives in the embrace of technology's wonders. Let us step into the future with hope and determination, knowing that a balanced and mindful coexistence with technology is within our reach, enriching our lives and the world we share.